NUCLEAR ENERGY

Chris Oxlade

Heinemann
LIBRARY

Chicago, Illinois

www.heinemannraintree.com
Visit our website to find out
more information about
Heinemann-Raintree books.

To order:

☎ Phone 888-454-2279
💻 Visit www.heinemannraintree.com
to browse our catalog and order online.

Edited by Louise Galpine and Laura Knowles
Designed by Philippa Jenkins
Original illustrations © Capstone Global Library
    Limited 2012
Picture research by Mica Brancic
Originated by Capstone Global Library Limited
Printed and bound in China by CTPS

15 14 13 12 11
10 9 8 7 6 5 4 3 2 1

Library of Congress Cataloging-in-Publication Data
Oxlade, Chris.
  Nuclear energy / Chris Oxlade.
     p. cm.—(Tales of invention)
  Includes bibliographical references and index.
  ISBN 978-1-4329-4879-5 (hc)—ISBN 978-1-4329-
4888-7 (pb) 1. Nuclear energy—Juvenile literature. I.
Title.
  TK9148.O94 2012
  621.48—dc22   2010036496

Acknowledgments
We would like to thank the following for permission to
reproduce photographs: Alamy pp. **16** (© Vespasian),
27 (© imagebroker); Corbis pp. **9** (© Bettmann), **11**
(© Bettmann), **15** (© Swim Ink), **20** (Sygma/© Igor
Kostin), **23** (© Underwood & Underwood), **26** (© Roger
Ressmeyer); Getty Images pp. **7** (Hulton Archive/Topical
Press Agency), **8** (MPI), **10** (Time & Life Pictures/
Los Alamos National Laboratory), **12** (Roger Viollet),
13 (Time & Life Pictures/Marie Hansen), **14** (Hulton
Archive/Jimmy Sime), **18** (Hulton Archive/Keystone/
Terry Fincher), **19** (Time & Life Pictures/Bill Pierce), **21**
(Patrick Landmann), **22** (The Image Bank/Sue Floo), **25**
(AFP Photo); Shutterstock p. **5** (© Martin Muránsky).

Cover photograph of an interior of a nuclear device
with technicians, Fort Belvoir, Virginia, reproduced with
permission of Corbis/© Underwood & Underwood.

We would like to thank Peter Smithurst for his
invaluable help in the preparation of this book.

Every effort has been made to contact copyright holders
of material reproduced in this book. Any omissions will
be rectified in subsequent printings if notice is given to
the publisher.

Disclaimer
All the Internet addresses (URLs) given in this book
were valid at the time of going to press. However, due
to the dynamic nature of the Internet, some addresses
may have changed, or sites may have changed or
ceased to exist since publication. While the author
and publisher regret any inconvenience this may cause
readers, no responsibility for any such changes can be
accepted by either the author or the publisher.

CONTENTS

Look for these boxes

Any words appearing in the text in bold, **like this**, are explained in the glossary.

Biographies

These boxes tell you about the life of inventors, the dates when they lived, and their important discoveries.

Setbacks

Here we tell you about the experiments that didn't work, the failures, and the accidents.

EUREKA!

These boxes tell you about important events and discoveries, and what inspired them.

TIMELINE

2011—The timeline shows you when important discoveries and inventions were made.

Everything around you is made from extremely tiny building blocks called **atoms**.

All about atoms

Atoms are so tiny that one million of them put side by side would be only as wide as a hair on your head. There are more than 100 different types of atom (such as carbon atoms or hydrogen atoms). Each type of atom is called an **element**. Carbon, hydrogen, and oxygen are different elements.

Nuclear reactions

In the middle of an atom is a **nucleus**. Energy is released when the nucleus of an atom breaks up, or when two nuclei join together. These changes are called **nuclear reactions**.

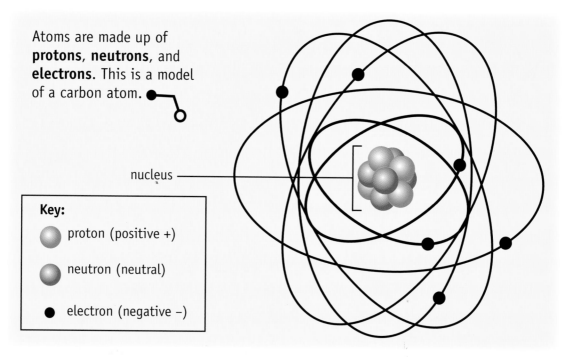

Atoms are made up of **protons**, **neutrons**, and **electrons**. This is a model of a carbon atom.

nucleus

Key:

proton (positive +)

neutron (neutral)

electron (negative –)

These huge cooling towers are part of a nuclear power station.

What is nuclear energy?

Nuclear energy is the energy that comes from atoms when they break up or join together. Scientists have invented ways of capturing this energy and using it to make electricity. We use electricity for many things, such as lighting, heating, working gadgets, and running trains. Scientists have also invented bombs that use nuclear energy to explode.

EUREKA!

In 1910 English scientist Ernest Rutherford was testing how **particles** passed through gold foil. Most went straight through, but a few bounced back. Rutherford was amazed. He realized that atoms in the foil must be made mostly of space, with a small nucleus in the middle that the particles had bounced off of.

5

1896—Marie and Pierre Curie discover **radiation** (see page 6)

THEORIES AND DISCOVERIES

Some materials give out **particles** that whizz along at high speed. Others give out rays like light, but invisible. These particles and rays are called **radiation**. Materials that give out radiation are called **radioactive**. Scientists Marie and Pierre Curie discovered radiation in 1896.

In 1939 two German scientists, Otto Hahn and Fritz Strassman, discovered that when an **atom** of **uranium** is hit by a **neutron**, it splits in two. The Austrian scientist Lise Meitner helped to explain how uranium atoms split up. She gave this **nuclear reaction** the name "**fission**."

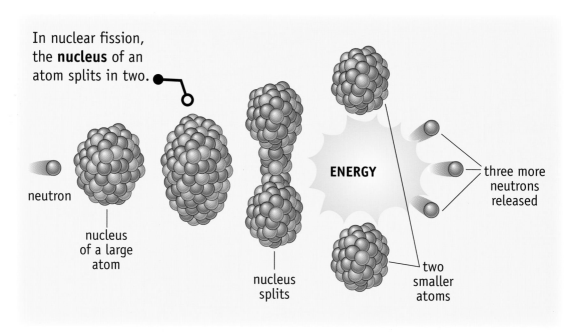

In nuclear fission, the **nucleus** of an atom splits in two.

neutron

nucleus of a large atom

nucleus splits

ENERGY

three more neutrons released

two smaller atoms

Chain reactions

Scientists soon discovered that when a uranium atom splits up, it releases neutrons as well as radioactivity. They realized that these neutrons would make other uranium atoms split up, producing even more neutrons. This is known as a **chain reaction**.

Otto Hahn *(1879-1968)*

Otto Hahn was in born Frankfurt, Germany. He worked on chemical weapons during World War I (1914–18), before returning to studying science. He discovered nuclear fission in 1939 in partnership with Fritz Strassman. Hahn was awarded the Nobel Prize for Chemistry in 1944. After World War II, he campaigned against the use of **nuclear weapons**.

1908—Ernest Rutherford wins the Nobel Prize for his research into radioactive materials

THE ATOMIC BOMB

In the early 1930s, the Nazi party, led by Adolf Hitler, took power in Germany. Many Jewish scientists, including Leo Szilard, Albert Einstein, and Lise Meitner, fled from Germany at this time. They did not feel safe under Nazi rule.

In 1939 Szilard created the first controlled nuclear **chain reaction** in a laboratory. He realized that if enough of one particular type of **uranium** was used, an uncontrolled nuclear chain reaction would occur. This could be used to make an extremely powerful **atomic bomb**.

Warning

Einstein warned the U.S. president, Franklin D. Roosevelt, that Germany might build an atomic bomb. So the U.S. government set up a project to research nuclear chain reactions. When the United States entered World War II in 1941, the government decided to build an atomic bomb.

-2-

The United States has only very poor ores of uranium in moderate quantities. There is some good ore in Canada and the former Czechoslovakia, while the most important source of uranium is Belgian Congo.

In view of this situation you may think it desirable to have some permanent contact maintained between the Administration and the group of physicists working on chain reactions in America. One possible way of achieving this might be for you to entrust with this task a person who has your confidence and who could perhaps serve in an inofficial capacity. His task might comprise the following:

a) to approach Government Departments, keep them informed of the further development, and put forward recommendations for Government action, giving particular attention to the problem of securing a supply of uranium ore for the United States;

b) to speed up the experimental work,which is at present being carried on within the limits of the budgets of University laboratories, by providing funds, if such funds be required, through his contacts with private persons who are willing to make contributions for this cause, and perhaps also by obtaining the co-operation of industrial laboratories which have the necessary equipment.

I understand that Germany has actually stopped the sale of uranium from the Czechoslovakian mines which she has taken over. That she should have taken such early action might perhaps be understood on the ground that the son of the German Under-Secretary of State, von Weizsäcker, is attached to the Kaiser-Wilhelm-Institut in Berlin where some of the American work on uranium is now being repeated.

Yours very truly,

A. Einstein

(Albert Einstein)

This is a page from Einstein's warning letter to the U.S. president.

1910—Ernest Rutherford discovers that **atoms** have a **nucleus** (see page 5)

The Manhattan Project

The United States' atomic bomb project became known as the Manhattan Project. The Manhattan scientists had to invent a way of setting off a chain reaction when they wanted it. They also had to invent a way to make the nuclear explosive for the bomb, which was to be made of uranium and **plutonium**.

EUREKA!

Leo Szilard was the first person to think of the idea of a nuclear chain reaction. The idea came into his head in September 1933, as he was walking to work in London, England. It was several years before nuclear **fission** was discovered.

9

The first reactor

Enrico Fermi and Leo Szilard invented the first **nuclear reactor**, the Chicago Pile-1 (CP-1). The first-ever nuclear chain reaction took place inside CP-1 in December 1942. Lessons learned from CP-1 helped to build two bigger reactors that produced enough plutonium fuel for a bomb.

Building the bomb

In 1943 a laboratory was set up in Los Alamos, New Mexico, to make the atomic bomb. The scientists used plutonium fuel surrounded by **high explosive**. The explosive started the chain reaction. The first bomb was tested in July 1945. It created an intense flash of light and a blast of heat, and then a **shock wave** arrived with a loud roar. A huge mushroom-shaped cloud rose into the sky.

Here, workers involved in the Manhattan Project pose for a photograph before performing a test explosion.

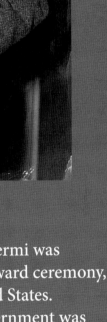

Enrico Fermi *(1901–1954)*

Enrico Fermi was born in Rome, Italy. In 1938 Fermi was awarded the Nobel Prize for Physics. After the award ceremony, he and his wife moved immediately to the United States. They moved because at that time the Italian government was anti-Jewish, and Fermi feared for the safety of his Jewish wife. He was asked to join the Manhattan Project, and he built the CP-1 nuclear reactor. After World War II, Fermi argued against developing a new type of nuclear bomb, the **hydrogen bomb**.

11

1930s—Scientists bombard atoms with **neutrons** to see what happens

The **Allies** defeated Germany in April 1945, but Japan fought on. The United States decided to drop an **atomic bomb** on a Japanese city to try to force Japan to surrender. Some of the Manhattan Project scientists, including Leo Szilard, were against the plan. They had seen the bomb's terrible destructive power.

Hiroshima and Nagasaki

An atomic bomb was dropped on the Japanese city of Hiroshima on August 6, 1945. Those who survived described a blinding flash of light and intense heat, followed by a powerful **shock wave**. Around 70,000 people died instantly. Tens of thousands more died afterward from their injuries, or from **radiation sickness** or disease. Three days later another bomb fell, this time on Nagasaki, Japan. Japan surrendered a few days later.

A huge mushroom cloud was produced by the atomic bomb dropped on Hiroshima.

Setbacks

In the United States, scientists were shocked by the events at Hiroshima. Albert Einstein said, "If I had known they were going to do this, I would have become a shoemaker."

1933—Albert Einstein flees Nazi Germany for the United States (see page 8)

1933—Leo Szilard flees to the United Kingdom, where he thinks of the idea of a nuclear **chain reaction** (see page 8)

Robert Oppenheimer (1904–1967)

Robert Oppenheimer was born in New York City. In 1942 he became
director of the Manhattan Project, and he gathered the best scientists
to work on the atomic bomb. After World War II he was head of the
U.S. Atomic Energy Commission. Members of this organization, including
Oppenheimer, voted against developing a more powerful **hydrogen bomb**.

1937—Leo Szilard
moves to the United
States to work at
Columbia University

1938—Enrico
Fermi wins the
Nobel Prize
for Physics
(see page 11)

1939—Strassman and
Hahn discover nuclear
fission. Szilard realizes
that an atomic bomb is
possible (see pages 6–8).

The Cold War

After World War II, the eastern half of Europe was **occupied** by the armies of the **Soviet Union**. The western half was occupied by the Allies, including the United States and the United Kingdom. These two sides became bitter rivals for the next 50 years, a period that is known as the Cold War. Each side built thousands of **nuclear weapons** that could be delivered directly by plane, or from far away by long-range **missile**, from land or sea. Governments published information leaflets about what to do in case of a nuclear attack.

Here, British troops are practicing for the launch of a nuclear missile in 1958.

1941—The United States enters World War II. The government orders an atomic bomb (see pages 8 and 9).

1942—The Manhattan Project is set up. The first-ever nuclear chain reaction takes place at the Chicago Pile-1 (CP-1) **reactor** (see pages 9 and 10).

1944—Otto Hahn is awarded the Nobel Prize for Chemistry (see page 7)

EUREKA!

The hydrogen bomb, also called the H-bomb, is many times more powerful than the atomic bomb. It works by joining hydrogen **atoms** together. This **nuclear reaction** is known as nuclear **fusion**. It was scientists Edward Teller and Stanislaw Ulam who realized that an atomic bomb could be used to create the high temperatures needed to set off a hydrogen bomb. Teller became known as "father of the H-bomb." The first hydrogen bomb was tested in 1952.

This poster was made in 1951, to try to prepare people in case of an attack.

The threat of war

The closest the two sides came to war was in 1962. The Soviet Union installed nuclear weapons in Cuba. This was within firing range of the United States. Fortunately, the sides found a political answer to the crisis. The Cold War finally came to an end when the Soviet Union collapsed in 1991.

15

1945—The first-ever nuclear bomb is tested in New Mexico (see page 10). Atomic bombs are dropped on the Japanese cities of Hiroshima and Nagasaki (see page 12).

1950s—The Soviet Union begins building nuclear submarines (see pages 22–23)

After World War II, scientists began to think about peaceful ways of using nuclear energy for producing power. The knowledge they learned from making **atomic bombs** helped. But for producing power, they needed to control a nuclear **chain reaction**—making it go faster or slower, or stopping it completely. And they had to capture the energy from the reaction and turn it into electricity. This is the work of a **nuclear reactor**.

The EBR-1 reactor is now a museum near Idaho Falls.

EUREKA!

The very first time electricity was generated from nuclear energy was in 1951. The reactor was the Experimental Breeder Reactor-1 (EBR-1) at Idaho Falls, Idaho. It produced enough electricity to light up its own building!

1951—Electricity is generated for the first time by a nuclear reactor

1952—First **hydrogen bomb** tested in the U.S. (see page 15)

1954—Electricity is generated by nuclear power for public use for the first time (see page 18)

1954—The first nuclear submarine, the USS *Nautilus*, is launched (see page 23)

1950

1955

How does a nuclear reactor work?

In the center of a nuclear reactor is the reactor **core**. This is where the chain reaction happens in the **nuclear fuel**. Also in the core is a material called a moderator. This slows down the **neutrons** released when **atoms** split up, so that the neutrons will cause other atoms to split. There are also **control rods** made from a material that absorbs neutrons. When the control rods are pushed into the core, they slow or stop the chain reaction.

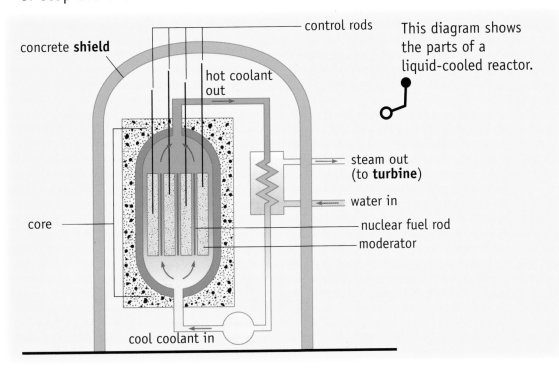

control rods

concrete **shield**

hot coolant out

This diagram shows the parts of a liquid-cooled reactor.

steam out (to **turbine**)

water in

core

nuclear fuel rod

moderator

cool coolant in

A liquid called **coolant** flows around the core. It gets heated up by the **radiation** from the core, then flows out, carrying heat away. After being cooled, it returns to the core again, just like the cooling system in a car engine.

1956—The Calder Hall nuclear power station opens in the United Kingdom (see page 18)

1957—The Shippingport nuclear power station opens in Pennsylvania (see page 18)

Generating electricity

At a nuclear power station, the coolant from a nuclear reactor heats water, making the water boil to make steam (see the diagram on page 17). The steam goes along pipes to **turbines**, making the turbines spin. The turbines turn electricity **generators**.

The first nuclear power station that generated electricity for homes and factories was opened in 1954 in the **Soviet Union**. Other early power stations opened at Calder Hall in the United Kingdom in 1956, and at Shippingport in Pennsylvania in 1957.

Here, control rods are being installed at the Calder Hall nuclear reactor in 1956.

1960—The first nuclear-powered aircraft carrier, the USS *Enterprise*, is launched (see page 23)

1962—The Soviet Union places nuclear **missiles** on the island of Cuba (see page 15)

The Three Mile Island nuclear power plant was damaged in a nuclear accident in 1979.

Reactor safety

Nuclear fuel gives off radiation during a **nuclear reaction**. Radiation is extremely harmful; it can cause **radiation sickness**, which can kill people. So a nuclear reactor has an automatic safety system that shuts itself down in the event of any problems. It is also covered with a concrete **shield** to stop radiation from leaking out.

Setbacks

On March 28, 1979, the Three Mile Island nuclear power plant, near Harrisburg, Pennsylvania, developed a serious problem. Some cooling water escaped from the reactor's cooling system. Half the reactor core got so hot that it melted. Steam and hydrogen gas escaped into the air, carrying harmful **radioactive** material with it. This showed that nuclear power stations were not as safe as people thought. Several reactors of similar design were closed down because of this.

Disaster at Chernobyl

The Chernobyl nuclear power station, near the city of Chernobyl in the Ukraine, was the site of the worst accident in nuclear energy's history. On April 26, 1986, engineers began testing the pumps on the reactor's cooling system. But they made mistakes, and the reactor began to run out of control. The reactor produced so much heat that the core exploded, blowing off the reactor shield.

It took nine days for firefighters to put out the fires and to stop radioactive materials from leaking. Thirty-two plant workers and firefighters died from radiation sickness.

After the Chernobyl disaster, helicopters were used to spray a sticky substance onto the ground. This helped stop the radioactive material from spreading in the air.

Today, the town of Prypyat, near Chernobyl, is deserted.

Setbacks

During the experiments at Chernobyl, too many of the 23,000 control rods were lowered, and the reactor began to shut down. Engineers raised the rods again, but they also switched off the automatic shutdown system. A few minutes later, the reactor was out of control.

Spreading radiation

A cloud of radioactive dust spread in the wind. There was 100 times more radiation than there had been at Hiroshima or Nagasaki. Some dust settled locally, causing high levels of radioactivity. Hundreds of thousands of people were evacuated, but dozens developed radiation sickness.

Eventually, the whole reactor was encased in concrete to stop further radiation leaks. The area around the reactor is now wasteland, and the soil is still radioactive today.

21

1979—An accident happens at the Three Mile Island nuclear power station in Pennsylvania (see page 19)

NUCLEAR ENERGY AT SEA

There are around 130 nuclear-powered ships in the world. Most of them are submarines. The **nuclear fuel** in a submarine lasts for many years before it has to be replaced. Another advantage is that nuclear power plants in submarines don't give out exhaust fumes or need a supply of air, as the diesel engines in normal submarines do. So nuclear submarines can stay submerged for months at a time.

Setbacks

The **Soviet Union** built its first nuclear submarines in the late 1950s. They were called the Project 627 submarines. There were several serious accidents on the submarines, caused by **radiation** leaks and reactors melting down.

This is a nuclear-powered ice breaker ship in the Arctic.

1982—The Tokamak **Fusion** Test Reactor (TFTR) begins operating (see page 25)

1983—Fusion experiments begin at the joint European Torus (JET) (see page 25)

1980   1985

This photo shows the launch of an early U.S. Navy nuclear submarine in 1959.

Ship reactors

Nuclear submarines have a small **nuclear reactor**, but it works just like the reactor in a nuclear power station. The heat from the **coolant** makes steam that drives **turbines**. The turbines turn the ship's propellers, as well as **generators** for the ship's electricity.

Work began on using nuclear energy for naval ships in the early 1950s. The first nuclear submarine was the USS *Nautilus* of the U.S. Navy, which was launched in 1954. By the end of the Cold War (see page 14), there were more than 400 nuclear-powered submarines in operation.

The first nuclear-powered aircraft carrier was the USS *Enterprise* of the U.S. Navy, launched in 1960. It has eight separate nuclear reactors.

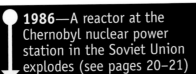

1986—A reactor at the Chernobyl nuclear power station in the Soviet Union explodes (see pages 20–21)

FUSION ENERGY

Nuclear **fusion** is when two **isotopes** of an **element** join together to make a larger **atom** of a different element. Nuclear fusion takes place in the center of the Sun. Here, under intense temperature and pressure, two isotope of hydrogen are fused to make one atom of helium. As they fuse, they release a huge amount of energy. This process also happens in **hydrogen bombs**.

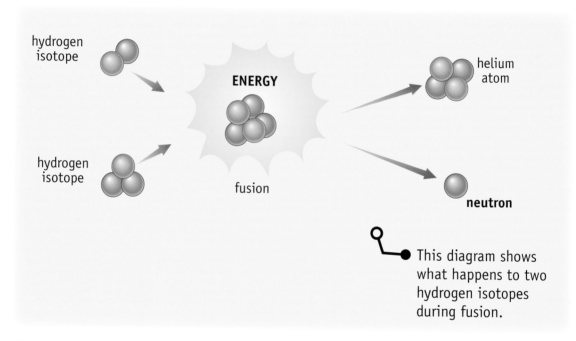

hydrogen isotope

ENERGY

helium atom

hydrogen isotope

fusion

neutron

This diagram shows what happens to two hydrogen isotopes during fusion.

Fusion reactors

Scientists are working on fusion **reactors**, but making fusion happen is not easy. A fusion reactor could produce many times more energy than a **fission** reactor. Another advantage of fusion is that it does not create large amounts of **radioactive waste**.

1991—The Soviet Union splits up, ending the Cold War (see page 15)

This is the JET experimental fusion reactor.

Heat for fusion

On Earth, fusion only happens at a temperature of about 100 million degrees Celsius (180 million degrees Fahrenheit). That is six times hotter than the center of the Sun. Heating the fuel in a reactor to this sort of temperature is extremely difficult. Scientists have built experimental fusion reactors, such as the Tokamak Fusion Test Reactor (TFTR) in the United States, and the Joint European Torus (JET) in the United Kingdom. These reactors have made fusion happen, but only for a tiny fraction of a second.

Setbacks

In 1989 scientists Martin Fleischmann and Stanley Pons claimed they had made fusion happen at room temperature, which is known as "cold fusion." However, they could not prove that fusion had happened, and no other scientist has managed to get the same results.

1997—JET breaks a world record by producing 16 megawatts of fusion power

Today, around 15 percent of the world's energy is produced in nuclear power stations. The greatest drawback of nuclear energy is **radioactive waste**, such as old fuel rods from **reactors**. Some of this waste stays **radioactive** for thousands of years. Storing the waste until it is safe remains a huge problem.

However, nuclear power stations do not produce as much carbon dioxide, which contributes to **global warming**. So some countries that banned nuclear energy in the past, such as Sweden and Italy, are now planning new reactors.

Nuclear disarmament

Since the Cold War ended in the 1980s, thousands of **nuclear weapons** have been destroyed. This is known as nuclear disarmament. But thousands of weapons still exist. Some countries keep these weapons as deterrents—in other words, to prevent other countries from attacking them.

These used fuel rods from nuclear reactors are being stored underwater in a special tank in France.

This new nuclear waste facility is being built in Germany.

A fusion future?

At the moment, scientists from many countries are building the International Thermonuclear Experimental Reactor (ITER) in France. This **fusion** reactor is a big step on the path to fusion energy. If the scientists can invent ways to overcome the problems they face, in a few decades we could have an almost limitless supply of energy that takes us into the far future.

Setbacks

There are international agreements that ban some countries from developing nuclear energy technology. This is because other countries fear that these countries might build and use nuclear weapons.

TIMELINE

1896
Radiation is discovered

1908
Ernest Rutherford wins the Nobel Prize for his research into **radioactive** materials

1910
Ernest Rutherford discovers that **atoms** have a **nucleus**

1944
Otto Hahn is awarded the Nobel Prize for Chemistry

1942
The Manhattan Project is set up. Robert Oppenheimer is made director.

1942
The first nuclear chain reaction takes place at the Chicago Pile-1 (CP-1) **reactor**

1945
The first-ever atomic bomb is tested in New Mexico

1945
Atomic bombs are dropped on the Japanese cities of Hiroshima and Nagasaki

1950s
The **Soviet Union** begins building nuclear submarines

1979
An accident happens at the Three Mile Island nuclear power station in Pennsylvania

1962
The Soviet Union puts nuclear **missiles** on the island of Cuba

1960
The first nuclear-powered aircraft carrier, the USS *Enterprise*, is launched

1982
The Tokamak **Fusion** Test reactor (TFTR) begins operating

1983
Fusion experiments begin at the Joint European Torus (JET)

1986
A reactor at the Chernobyl nuclear power station in the Soviet Union explodes

1930s
Scientists bombard atoms with **neutrons** to see what happens

1933
Albert Einstein flees Nazi Germany for the United States

1933
Leo Szilard flees to the United Kingdom, where he thinks of the idea of a nuclear **chain reaction**

1941
The United States enters World War II. The U.S. government decides to build an atomic bomb.

1939
Hahn and Strassman discover nuclear **fission**. Leo Szilard realizes an **atomic bomb** is possible.

1938
Enrico Fermi is awarded the Nobel Prize for Physics

1951
Electricity is generated for the first time by a nuclear reactor

1952
The first **hydrogen bomb** is tested in the United States

1954
Electricity is generated by nuclear power for public use for the first time

1957
The Shippingport nuclear power station opens in Pennsylvania

1956
The Calder Hall nuclear power station opens in the United Kingdom

1954
The first nuclear submarine, the USS *Nautilus*, is launched

1991
The Soviet Union splits up, ending the Cold War

1997
JET breaks a world record by producing 16 megawatts of fusion power

2010
Building work begins on the International Thermonuclear Experimental Reactor (ITER)

GLOSSARY

Allies United States, United Kingdom, Russia, and other countries that fought on the same side during World War II

atom smallest particle of any element. All materials are made up of atoms.

atomic bomb nuclear bomb that explodes when atoms split apart, releasing huge amounts of energy

chain reaction when one atom splitting up causes the atoms around it to split up, too

control rod rod that is lowered into the core of a nuclear reactor, which slows or stops the chain reaction in the nuclear fuel

coolant liquid or gas that carries heat away from the core of a nuclear reactor

core part of a reactor where nuclear reactions take place

electron tiny particle with a negative charge found outside an atom's nucleus

element single chemical unit, such as hydrogen or uranium

fission nuclear reaction in which the nucleus of an atom breaks up

fusion nuclear reaction in which the nuclei of two atoms join together

generator any device that produces electricity

global warming gradual warming of Earth's atmosphere caused mainly by gases released when we burn certain fuels

high explosive material that explodes very suddenly, causing a shock wave

hydrogen bomb nuclear bomb that explodes when atoms join together, releasing huge amounts of energy

isotope atom that is of the same element as another atom, but has a different number of neutrons

missile weapon sent to its target by remote control

neutron uncharged particle that is part of the nucleus of an atom

nuclear fuel material used in nuclear reactors and nuclear weapons that takes part in nuclear reactions

nuclear reaction when the nucleus of an atom breaks apart or two nuclei join together

nuclear reactor place where nuclear reactions take place, producing heat

nuclear weapon bomb that explodes because of nuclear reactions

nucleus (plural: nuclei) core of an atom, made up of protons and neutrons

occupied invaded and taken over

particle smallest unit of matter. Particles are the building blocks of atoms.

plutonium metal element that is radioactive, it is used as a fuel in nuclear reactors

proton positively charged particle that is part of the nucleus of an atom

radiation high-speed particles or rays (like light, but invisible) given off by radioactive materials

radiation sickness severe illness caused by radiation

radioactive describes a material that gives off radiation

radioactive waste waste material from nuclear reactors, such as old fuel

reactor see nuclear reactor

shield thick concrete or metal cover that surrounds a nuclear reactor to stop radiation from escaping

shock wave powerful wave of pressure that travels outward from an explosion

Soviet Union country that was made up of the countries under Russian control after World War II

turbine device that contains fans that spin around when gas or steam flows through them

uranium metal element that is radioactive, it is used as fuel in nuclear reactors

FIND OUT MORE

Books

Bodden, Valerie. *The Bombing of Hiroshima and Nagasaki* (*Days of Change*). Mankato, Minn.: Creative Education, 2008.

Oxlade, Chris. *Inventors' Secret Scrapbook* (*Crabtree Connections*). New York: Crabtree, 2011.

Oxlade, Chris. *Nuclear Power* (*Science in the News*). Mankato, Minn.: Smart Apple Media, 2010.

Websites

www.iaea.org
This is the website of the International Atomic Energy Agency, which works for the safe and peaceful use of nuclear energy.

www.iter.org
Visit this website to find out all about the ITER experimental fusion reactor.

www.pcf.city.hiroshima.jp
You can find out about the Hiroshima bomb at the Hiroshima Peace Museum website. Click on "English web site" at the top of the page.

A place to visit

National Museum of Nuclear Science and History
601 Eubank Boulevard SE at Southern Boulevard
Albuquerque, New Mexico 87123
www.nuclearmuseum.org
Visit this museum to learn more about the history of people discovering and using nuclear energy.

INDEX